9.84

Nature's Children

MOTHS

Bill Ivy

 Grolier

FACTS IN BRIEF

Classification of moths

Class: *Insecta* (insects)

Order: *Lepidoptera* (moths and butterflies)

Family: There are approximately 100 families of moths.

Species: Approximately 1 000 000 moth species have been named, roughly 15 000 of these are found in North America.

World distribution.   Moths are found in almost all areas of the world.

Habitat.   Varies with species.

Distinctive physical characteristics.   Thick furry body, antennae which are feathery or thread-like, dusty wings which are folded over the back when the moth is at rest.

Habits.   Most moths are active only at night, and are attracted by light.

Diet.   Varies with species.

Published originally as
"Getting to Know . . . Nature's Children."

This series is approved and recommended
by the Federation of Ontario Naturalists.

This library reinforced edition is available exclusively from:

Grolier Educational Corporation
Sherman Turnpike, Danbury, Connecticut 06816

Contents

Where They Live   Page 6

Who's Who?   Page 9

Moths Up Close   Page 10

Super Sight   Page 13

Other Senses   Page 14

Small Beginnings   Page 19

Curious Cats   Page 20

Dangerous Lives   Page 23

Preparing for Change   Page 24

A Great Mystery   Page 27

New Life   Page 28

Champion Flyers   Page 31

Measuring Up   Page 32

Now You See Them, Now You Don't   Page 35

Tiny Tigers   Page 36

Night Owls   Page 39

Winged Royalty   Page 40

A Taste for Trouble   Page 42

Friends in Deed   Page 44

Words to Know   Page 47

Index   Page 48

When someone mentions the word *moth,* what comes to mind? If you are like most people, you probably think of a drab little insect that is about as exciting as a slug! But did you know that many moths are as graceful and beautiful as butterflies? Even those that seem dull at first glance are often exquisitely patterned when seen up close.

Moths come in all sizes, shapes and colors. Some have a wingspan larger than your hand while others are so tiny that you can barely see them. The one thing they all have in common is that their life story is one of the most fascinating in nature. So if you have always thought of moths as boring, you are in for a surprise! Curious? Then read on.

The exquisite Luna Moth is found only in North America and is this continent's only swallow-tailed moth.

Where They Live

There are very few places in the world where moths do not live. They can be found in fields and woods, in scorching hot deserts and on cool mountain slopes. In North America alone there may be 15 000 different species! No one knows the exact number since new species are constantly being discovered.

Although moths far outnumber their more popular cousins, the butterflies, they are not as well known since most of them are creatures of the night.

The Pale Beauty Moth can be found all across Canada and in many parts of the United States.

Who's Who?

Have you ever wondered how you can tell the difference between a moth and a butterfly? Although it is not always easy to tell them apart, here are a few clues to help you:

— Most moths are active between dusk and dawn, while butterflies are only active during the day.

— While at rest, moths generally fold their wings flat over their backs; butterflies usually hold theirs upright and shut tight.

— Butterflies have a club at the tip of their antennae, while moths have feathery or thread-like antennae.

— Finally, moths have thicker, furrier bodies than butterflies and most of them are not as colorful.

The Ctenucha Moth can be found on grasses and flowers during the day.

Moths Up Close

Moths, like all insects, have six legs and three body parts: the head, thorax and abdomen. Most have two pairs of wings which are covered with millions of tiny colored scales. This is why moths—like their butterfly relatives—belong to a group of insects known as *Lepidoptera,* a Greek word which means "scaly winged."

The scales on a moth's wing overlap each other like the shingles on a roof and rub off as a fine dust if you touch them. They provide the wings with their colors and patterns and protect them from damage.

When the Io Moth opens its wings, two large eyespots appear. It is thought that these markings may frighten away enemies interested in a moth dinner.

Super Sight

The world must look quite different to moths than it does to us. Like all insects, a moth has not one but two sets of eyes. Most important are the two enormous *compound* eyes, made up of thousands of tiny, six-sided lenses. Under a microscope these strange eyes look like a honeycomb. Then, hidden in the hair behind the moth's feelers is a set of two small, simple eyes. No wonder moths have such excellent eyesight and can detect the slightest movement!

Again like other insects—and like us—moths can see in color. In fact, their eyes are sensitive to a color that we are unable to see—ultraviolet. Seeing ultraviolet is like adding bright orange to a gray picture. Ultraviolet is much more visible at night than most colors and many of the flowers moths feed on reflect it. The ability to see it is therefore very useful to moths since most of them feed at night.

The Promethea Moth is one of the few species in which the males and females do not look alike. This female is much more colorful than her blackish mate.

Other Senses

A moth's antennae act as a nose and are very sensitive to odors. This keen sense of smell helps moths find food, but probably its most important use is to help male moths find a mate. Female moths give off a scent that the males find irresistible. Some suitors can detect this perfume several kilometres (miles) away!

In a different way, a moth's sense of taste is as remarkable as its sense of smell: it is located in the soles of the moth's feet! By walking on a blossom, moths can immediately tell whether or not there is nectar inside. If so, they simply uncoil their long tube-like "tongue" and drink up!

Many moths can also hear. Using round drum-like membranes on their bodies, they can detect a variety of sounds including some of the high-pitched squeaks of a hunting bat. Incredibly, some moths seem to be able to imitate the bat's sounds. This confuses it and allows the moth to escape.

Opposite page:
If there is a female close by, these fern-like antennae will help this male Cecropia Moth track her down.

Fatal Attraction

Have you ever heard the expression, "like a moth to a flame?" It means to be irresistibly drawn to something, as moths are to light. Often, you can see large swarms of moths fluttering aimlessly around streetlights at night. What causes this strange behavior?

One theory is that moths navigate by the light of the moon. Since the moon is so far from the earth, its rays strike the ground parallel to each other. By keeping the angle of moonlight that hits its eyes the same, the moth keeps on course. However, with lights that are much closer, the rays radiate out like the spokes of a wheel. In order to keep these beams striking its eyes at the same angle, the moth must keep turning closer and closer to the light. Should this beacon happen to be a flame it's soon "lights out" for the unsuspecting moth!

This beautiful Haploa Moth is attracted to lights at night.

Small Beginnings

Like a bird, a moth begins its life as an egg. Of course, moths' eggs are much smaller than birds' eggs. Most, in fact are no bigger than the head of a pin. They come in various shapes and colors. They may be round or flat, cone- or barrel-shaped. Some are smooth while others are ribbed. Most are a plain brown, green or white color but some are spotted. In each case, the eggs are designed to blend in with their surroundings so that hungry creatures cannot find them.

When a female is ready to lay her eggs she finds a suitable spot. The majority glue their eggs either singly or in groups to the ground or onto leaves, plants, stems or bark. One female may lay as many as 10 000 eggs. Then her job is complete: she flies off and never sees her young.

Most eggs hatch within a week, but those laid in the fall may overwinter and hatch the following spring.

Cecropia Moth eggs.

Curious Cats

The first meal a newborn caterpillar, or larva, eats is often its own egg shell. The second is usually fresh leaves, although some larvae feed on fruit, seeds or wood. One species is particularly fond of apples—as you may already know if you have ever gone to bite into an apple and found yourself eye to eye with a "worm!"

The young larva has an incredible appetite and eats both day and night, stopping only for the briefest of rests. It grows very quickly and

One of our best-known caterpillars is that of the Isabella Tiger Moth, commonly known as the woolly bear. Its main claim to fame is its supposed ability to predict the weather. According to folklore the closer together the black bands are on each end of its body, the more severe the approaching winter will be. Unfortunately, the woolly bear is even less reliable at predicting the weather than our own weather forecasters.

soon it is too big for its skin. If you wear a coat that is too small, it will finally tear at the seams and this is what happens to the caterpillar. Its old skin splits down the back, and the larva crawls out wearing the new baggy skin that has grown underneath. This is known as molting and usually occurs five times before the caterpillar is fully grown. Each time the caterpillar's colors may be different and its body may even change shape as new parts are grown or lost.

Many caterpillars are smooth, while others are covered with warts and bumps. Several species are hairy. In fact, the word caterpillar comes from a Latin name meaning ''hairy cat.'' All caterpillars have six legs and up to five pairs of large claspers that they use for gripping. Although larvae have twelve tiny eyes they can probably only see well enough to tell light from dark. For this reason they must rely on their two antennae to help them find their way around.

Dangerous Lives

Life is very dangerous for moth larvae. Mice, chipmunks, frogs, snakes, spiders and birds all enjoy a meal of juicy fat caterpillars. A single pair of nesting birds may feed as many as a hundred caterpillars a day to their hungry nestlings! However, the caterpillars' most deadly enemies are the tiny wasps and flies that lay eggs on their bodies. These eggs soon hatch into tiny larvae that immediately begin to feed on their unfortunate hosts. The poor caterpillars are literally eaten alive!

Caterpillars have a variety of ways to protect themselves. A few species have poisonous hairs or spines, while others taste so bad that no animal would want to eat them. Still others have a dangerous-looking horn-like projection that they wave defiantly at intruders. Most caterpillars, however, rely on their ability to blend into their surroundings. Some are so well camouflaged that they are almost impossible to see.

Opposite page:
The amazing appetite of the Polyphemus Moth caterpillar has earned it a place in the Guinness Book of World Records. *In the first 48 hours of its life it eats about 86 000 times its own birthweight in food.*

Preparing for Change

When fully grown a moth larva stops eating and prepares for the next change of its life. It must now select a safe place to molt for the last time. Some species burrow into the ground while others crawl under loose bark, fallen leaves or rocks. Most spin strong silken cocoons around themselves for protection from enemies and bad weather. To do this, they use special glands near their mouth. Liquid silk is forced out through little nozzles known as spinnerets and quickly hardens into a slender thread.

Next, the caterpillar begins to shrink and shrivel and looks as if it is dying. When it finally sheds its skin, it is no longer a caterpillar but a strange mummy-like creature known as a pupa. The pupa's soft pale skin soon hardens and darkens. It is within this seemingly lifeless case that a miracle takes place.

The Cecropia Moth pupa spends the winter in a strong waterproof cocoon attached to a twig.

A Great Mystery

If you are every lucky enough to come across a pupa, look carefully at the outer surface and you will see the outline of the future moth's wings, legs and antennae. And yet, unbelievable as it may seem, there is nothing inside but a milky liquid. Somehow this mysterious liquid will gradually solidify into a fully formed moth.

Exactly how this incredible change takes place, no one fully understands. In some kinds of moths it takes only a few days. In others it may take over a year.

The word pupa means doll. Does this Regal Moth pupa look like a little doll wrapped in its blanket to you?

New Life

In order to begin its new life a moth must first break out of its cramped quarters. By expanding itself with air and tightening its muscles the moth splits its pupa shell and pulls itself out. Those in a cocoon have another barrier to break through. Some species use a built-in escape hatch. Others have special cutters that they use to clip their way to freedom. Many moths produce a fluid that dissolves the cocoon's silk fibers.

Once the moth is free it must find a safe place to hang. What a sorry looking sight it is with its damp swollen body and small crumpled wings! But then its wings begin to unfold. Gradually they expand to their full size, and the moth has only to wait for them to harden and dry before it can take to the air.

The moth has now reached its fourth and final stage and will change and grow no more. The most vital part of its life still lies ahead, however. It must now find a mate and start the whole cycle of life again.

Opposite page:
Free at last!
(Luna Moth)

Now that you know more about moths in general, let's take a closer look at a few of these fascinating insects.

Champion Flyers

Next time you see what appears to be a hummingbird darting from flower to flower, look again—it just might be a Hawk Moth. Like hummingbirds these incredible moths have extra long tongues that enable them to feed on the nectar of deep-throated flowers. Also like hummingbirds, they can hover in mid-air and can even fly backwards! With their tapered bodies and narrow wings, these streamlined insects are the fastest fliers in the moth world. Some species reach speeds of 60 kilometres (37 miles) per hour.

The Hawk Moth is also known as the Sphinx Moth because of its caterpillar's peculiar habit of resting motionless with its front end rearing up. In this pose it looks like a tiny copy of the world-famous Egyptian Sphinx.

Opposite page: *Many Hawk Moths are beautifully marked with brightly colored hindwings or large eyespots. The eyespots on this Blinded Sphinx Moth are easy to see.*

Measuring Up

Have you ever walked under a tree on a hot summer day and come face to face with a caterpillar dangling on a thread of silk? If so, you have already met the Geometer Moth's caterpillar, better known as the inchworm. Next time you see one, let it land on you and watch the curious way it moves. First it stretches its front end forward as far as it can. Next it grabs hold with its claspers and loops up the rest of its body to make both ends meet. Then it does the same thing again—and again and again and again.

If you can easily recognize Geometer Moth caterpillars by the odd way they move, how do you recognize the adults? By the way they don't move! Unlike the majority of moths, most members of this family rest with their wings spread out flat. Among the exceptions to this rule are the females of some species. Them, you recognize by the surprising fact that they do not have any wings at all!

Opposite page:
Unlike most Geometer Moths, Kent's Geometer Moth rests with its wings closed up over its back the way a butterfly does.

Now You See Them, Now You Don't

The Underwing Moths are masters of camouflage. During the day they rest on tree trunks or rocks where they blend in so well with their surroundings that they are almost invisible. Hidden beneath their drab front wings, however, are colorful hindwings that are usually marked with bands of red, yellow, black or orange.

This eye-catching arrangement probably helps these moths live longer. In flight their underwings flash color, but once the moth lands the color suddenly disappears. Any enemy that may have been chasing one will probably fly right past in search of the bright markings. How's that for a vanishing act?

The Once-married Underwing.

35

Tiny Tigers

It is easy to see how the Tiger Moth, with its bold black and white or yellow markings, got its name. These beautiful moths live in the woods and are usually active only at night. During the day they rest on the bark of trees against which their brilliant colors are very noticeable. But doesn't that make them easy prey for hungry insectivores? Easy maybe, but not very appetizing. A captured Tiger Moth gives off an awful-smelling liquid that usually convinces its enemies to leave it alone. The brilliant color may actually serve as a warning for potential diners to look elsewhere.

Although you may never have seen a Tiger Moth, you have probably crossed paths with its caterpillar. It has a fuzzy body and is commonly seen running along the ground. If you pick it up it will roll into a ball and play dead.

Great Tiger Moth.

Night Owls

If you were to search the woods with a flashlight at night, you might find a pair of tiny eyes glowing eerily in the dark. Should this happen to you, don't be afraid. They are most likely the eyes of an Owlet Moth. Of course, you can now guess how these moths got their name. Like owls, they have eyes that shine when light strikes them, and most are active at night. At rest during the day, Owlet Moths hold their wings roof-like over their bodies, resembling tiny triangles. They are sometimes called Miller Moths because the scales on their wings rub off like fine flour.

There are more Owlet Moths in the world than any other species.

Owlet Moth caterpillars are often mistaken for worms. Most pupate in the ground and take up to two years to complete their life cycle. One group, known as cutworms, have the annoying habit of nipping off tender plant shoots at night. Needless to say, they are not very popular with gardeners!

Opposite page: *The tiny 8-spotted Forester Moth is one of our most beautiful Owlet Moths.*

Winged Royalty

Meet the grandest family of the moth world, the Silk or Emperor Moths. These royal creatures are among our largest and most beautiful insects. Not only is their size impressive—some have a wingspan of over 15 centimetres (6 inches)—but their wings are works of art. Many have a transparent window in the middle of each hindwing and display large "peacock eyes" that seem to stare right at you. Their bodies are stocky and covered with thick hair. In flight, Silk Moths are often mistaken for bats.

If you have never seen a Silk Moth before, there is a good reason why. Not only are most species active only at night, but they have a very short lifespan. They do not eat once they become adults so that they can put all their time and energy into finding a mate, seeking out the right kind of tree and laying their eggs on it. They live only long enough to complete these tasks—usually one or two weeks.

Opposite page:
The Polyphemus Moth is named after the one-eyed Cyclops of Greek mythology. Why? Its large eyespots are the obvious answer.

A Taste for Trouble

While moths are generally harmless, the larvae of a few species can be a pest, especially those that eat the same foods as we do! Some burrow into fruit such as apples and peaches, while others attack fields of corn, grain and cotton. No less a problem are those that strip leaves off trees and plants. When they occur in large numbers, they can cause severe damage to forests.

Another common pest is known for its unusual diet. Have you ever taken a sweater out of the closet and discovered it had tiny holes in it? If so, the damage may have been the work of the Common Clothes Moth larvae, which have an appetite for wool, silk and fur. Many people mistakenly believe that the adult moths also eat clothes, but this is not true. In fact, they do not eat at all!

Many moths blend in so well with their surroundings that they are almost impossible to see. Can you spot the Hawk Moth in this picture?

Friends in Deed

Moths are not only fascinating but useful too. Many flowers that bloom at night depend upon them for survival. Plants cannot produce seeds without first being pollinated. As moths visit flowers to feed, some of the pollen rubs off the flowers onto their bodies and is carried to other plants. A few of our important crops are pollinated this way as well.

We also have the moth to thank for one of our most treasured luxuries—silk. The Silkworm Moth of Asia has been used for over 4000 years to produce this wonderful cloth. Its silk cocoon is carefully unravelled into one long strand which is then combined with other threads and woven into fabric.

Believe it or not, it takes over 50 000 cocoons to make a single kilogram (2 pounds) of silk! So if you ever have the pleasure of slipping into a silk shirt, or the next time you find a beautiful moth clinging to your window screen in the morning, consider what a poorer place this world would be without moths.

And if you are still not convinced, try discovering moths first hand. Shine a bright light on an outside wall at night and you will be amazed at the variety of moths that come. It is one of the best shows around and constantly changes as new moths emerge throughout the year.

Originally from China, the Cynthia Moth was introduced to North America as a possible silk producer.

Words to Know

Antennae   Sensory organs of insects, such as moths.

Camouflage   Coloring that makes an animal blend into the background.

Caterpillar   The second stage in a moth's life. Also called the *larva*.

Claspers   The grasping hooks that a caterpillar uses to hold on to things.

Compound eyes   Eyes that have many lenses instead of just one.

Cocoon   A strong silk case that a caterpillar spins around itself in preparation for the next, *pupa*, stage of its life.

Eyespots   Spots on the wings of some moths that look like a pair of eyes.

Gland   A part of the body where certain substances are made.

Insectivores   Animals that eat mainly insects.

Larva   The caterpillar stage of a moth's life.

Lepidoptera   The order of insects to which moths and butterflies belong.

Molt   To shed old skin or feathers to make way for new.

Pupa   The third stage in a moth's life during which it changes into its adult form.

Pupate   To go through the pupa stage.

Spinnerets   The part of the caterpillar's body that forms the silk threads with which it spins its cocoon.

Thorax   The part of a moth's body, behind the head, to which the wings and the legs are attached.

INDEX

adult moth, 10-16, 28, 31, 32, 35-41, 44
    antennae, 9, 14
    description, 9, 10, 30-41, 44
    diet, 13, 20, 31
    distribution, 6
    enemies, 14, 36
    eyes, 13
    feet, 14
    female, 14, 19
    habitat, 6
    lifespan, 40
    locomotion, 31
    male, 14, 19
    protection, 14, 35, 36
    senses, 13, 14
    tongue, 14, 31
    wings, 9, 10

caterpillar, 20, 21, 32
    antennae, 21
    change to pupa, 24
    description, 21, 32, 36, 39
    diet, 20, 39, 42
    enemies, 23
    locomotion, 32
    molting, 21, 24
    protection, 23, 36
    senses, 21

cocoon, 24, 28
Common Clothes Moth, 42

egg, 19
    description, 19
    hatching, 19
    protection, 19

Emperor Moth, 40

Hawk Moth, 31

inchworm, 32

larva. *See* caterpillar

Owlet Moth, 39

pupa, 24, 39
    change to adult, 28
    coming out, 28
    description, 27, 28

relatives, 6, 9, 10

Silkworm Moth, 44

Tiger Moth, 36

Underwing Moth, 35

woolly bear, 20

Cover Photo: Bill Ivy.
Photo Credits: All photos by Bill Ivy.

Printed and Bound in Italy by Lego SpA